WORD WINGS BOOKS
Published by Word Wings Publishing (Brisbane, Australia)

First edition, first published in Australia by Word Wings in 2017.

Text copyright © 2017 by J.R.McRae
Illustrations copyright © Claudia Emanuela Coppola
Illustration & Design © Takara Beech

The moral right of the author and illustrator has been asserted.
First edition, first Australian edition 2017.
All rights reserved.

Illustration & design by Kellie Farnham under nom de plume © Takara Beech

No part of this publication may be reproduced, stored in a retrieval system, or transmitted, in any form, or by any means, electrical, mechanical, photocopying, recording or otherwise without the prior written permission of the publisher or license permitting restricted copying. In Australia, such licences are issued by CAL.

National Library of Australia Cataloguing in Publication entry

Creator: McRae, J.R., author.
Title: Catching a dream / by J.R.McRae; pictures by Claudia Emanuela Coppola;
illustrator/designer: Takara Beech.

ISBN 978 1 925484 40 3 (paperback)
Target Audience: For older readers, YA and general readership.

Subjects: Dreams – Poetry.
Imagination in children.
Learning by discovery.
Child development.
Australian poetry.

Other Creators/Contributors: Coppola, Claudia Emanuela, illustrator.
Beech, Takara, illustrator, book designer.

wordwings.wix.com/publishing
https://www.facebook.com/WordWingsPublishing/

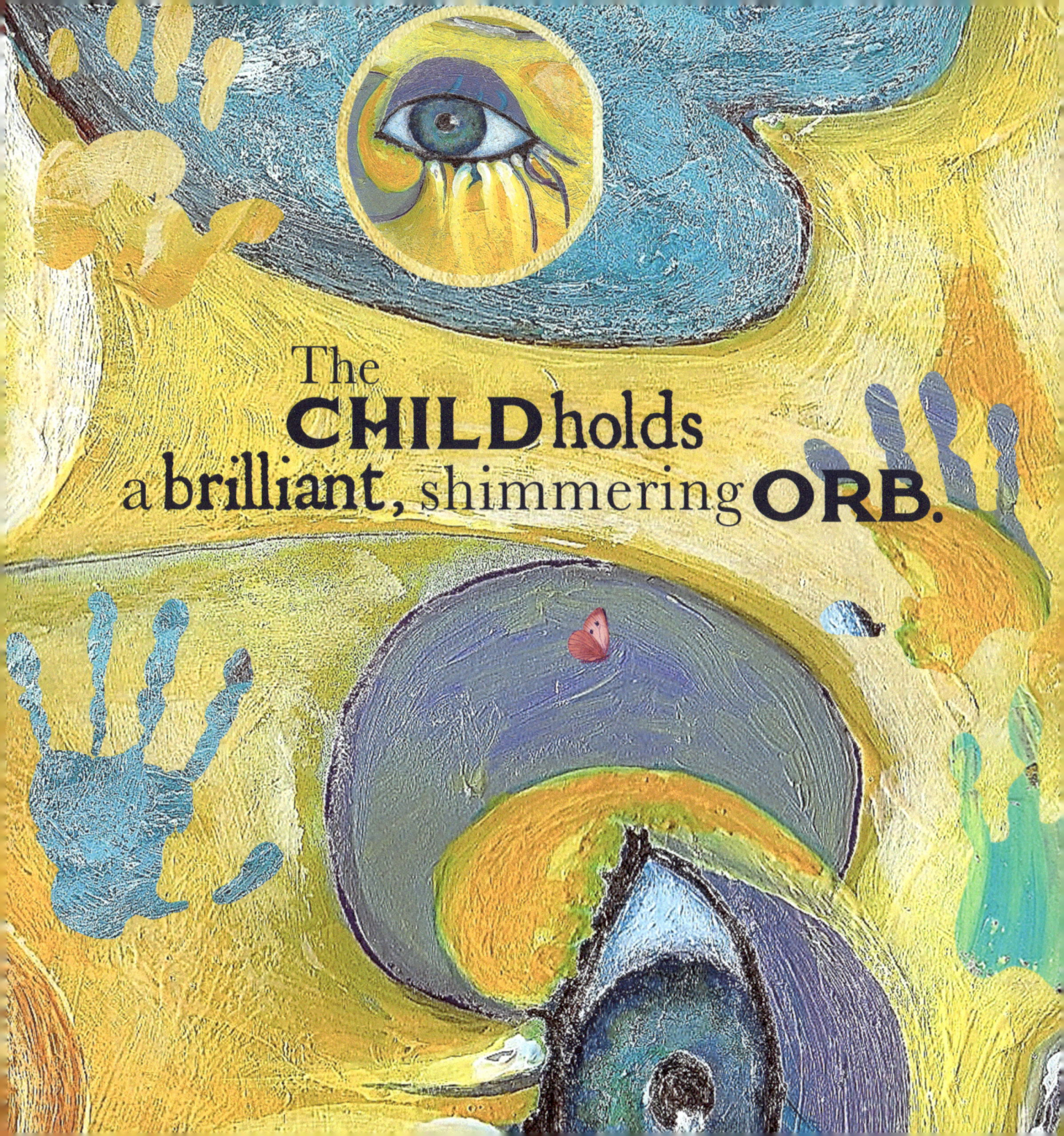

The
CHILD holds a cup,

Sees how it
fills up

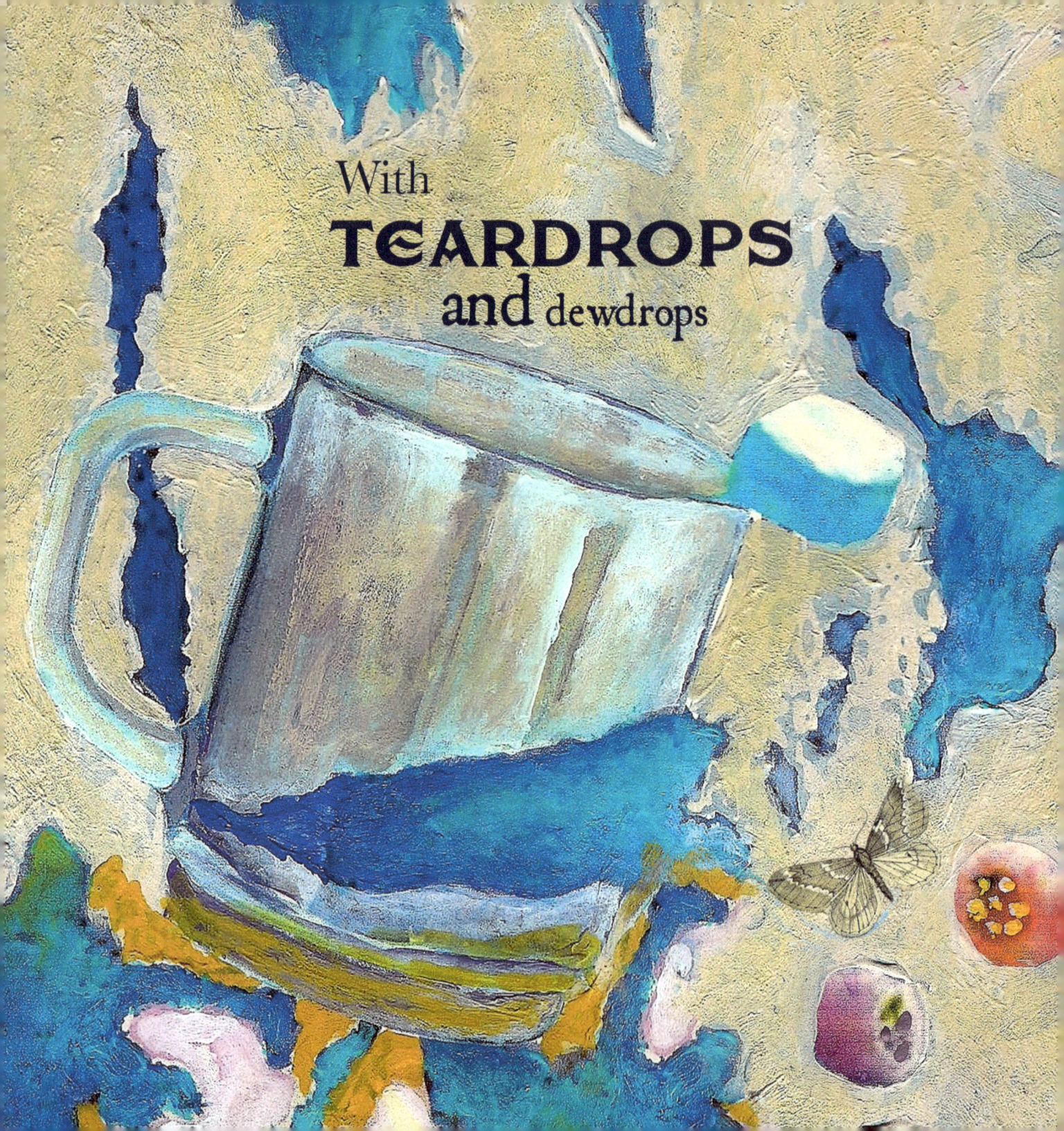

And bright coloured
candy drops!

The **CHILD** holds a bowl,

Tips it **up** so the whole

Empties
and
SPILLS
Ocean waves,
river rills.

The **CHILD** holds a **dream**,

The **CHILD** holds the hand of the **weathered,** old **MAN**

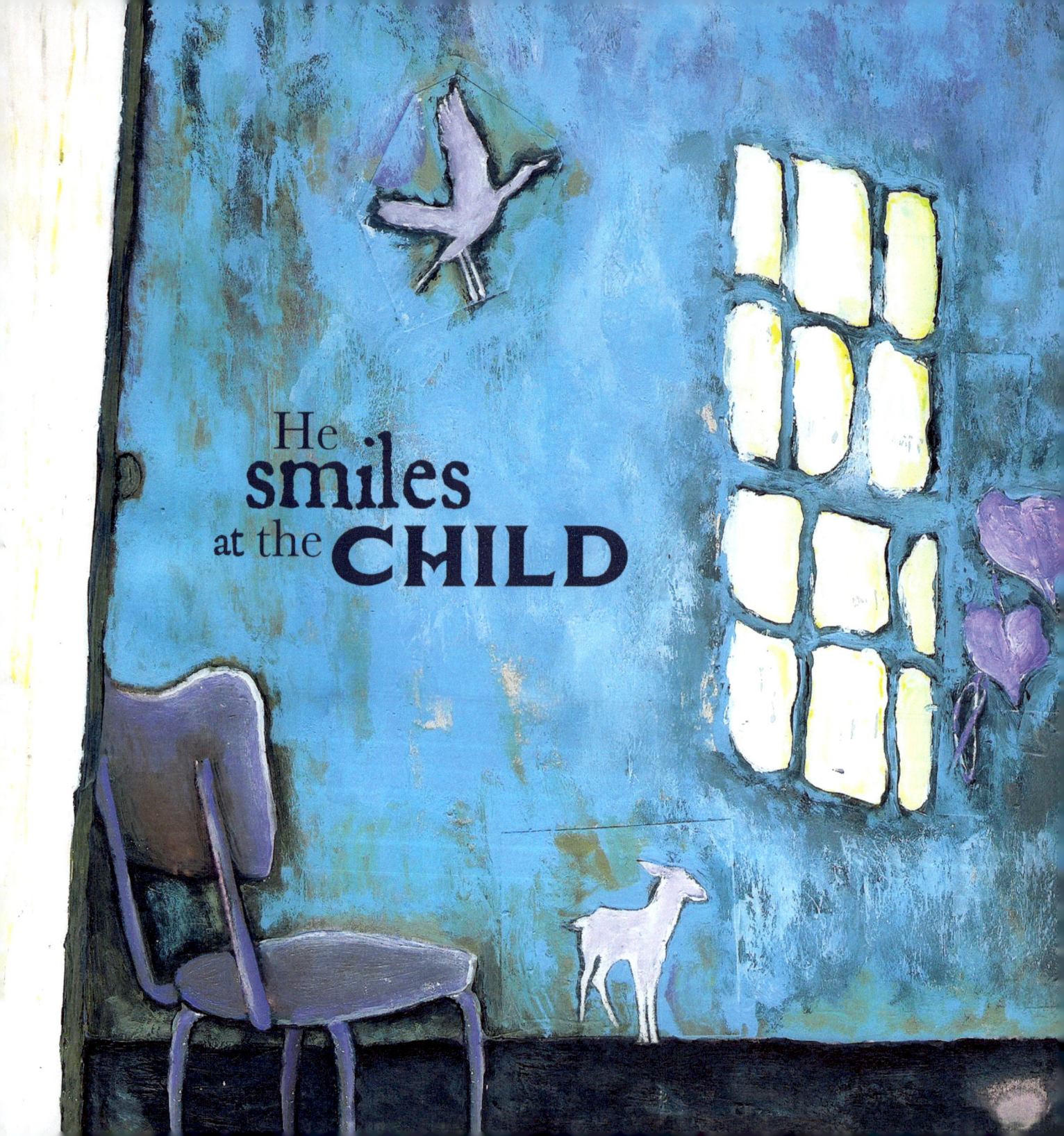

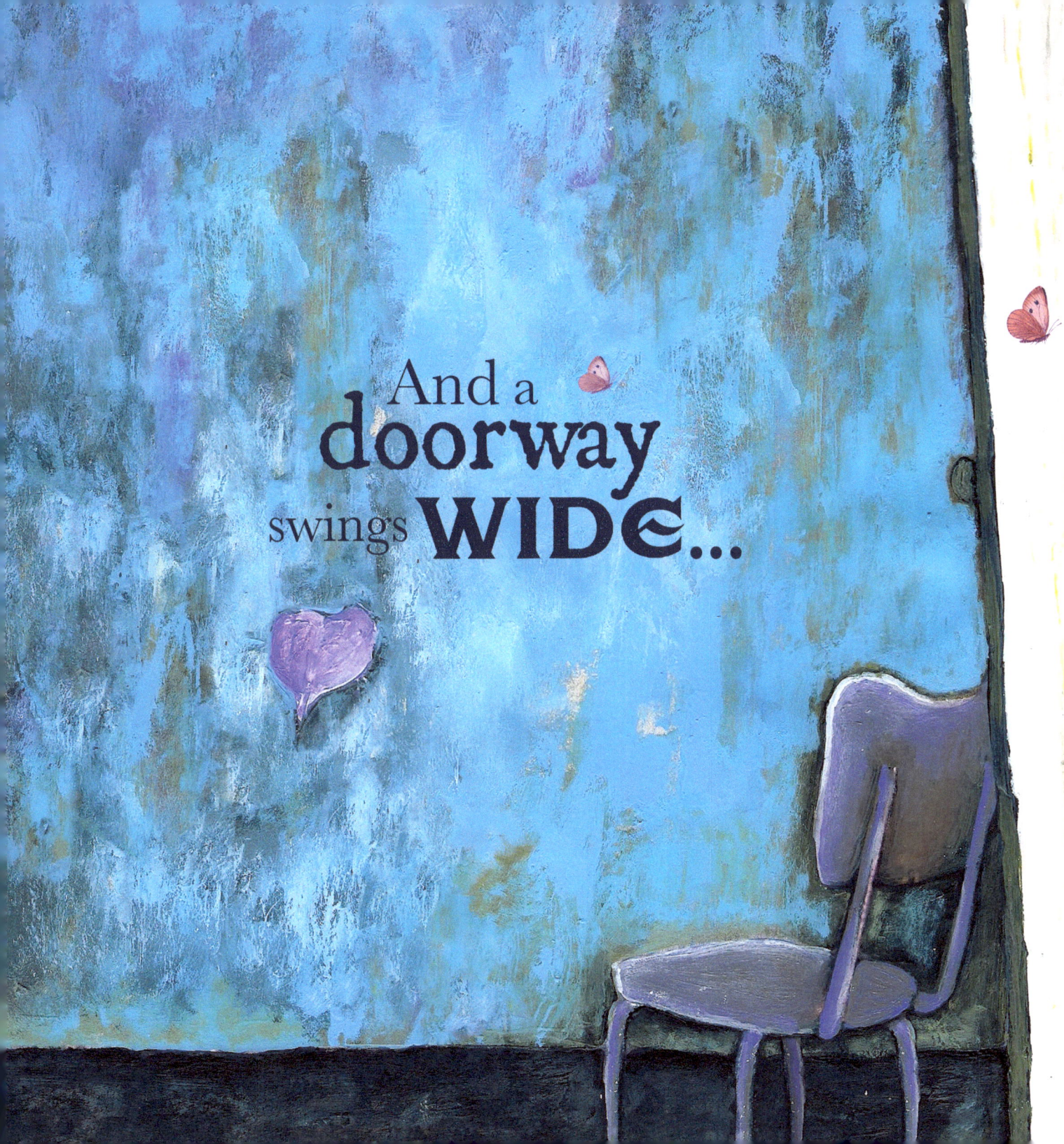

The child holds the SOUND

Of a voice soft as down,

A knowing that's growing INSIDE...

The CHILD lets go slowly and ventures outside...

J.R.Poulter once worked in a *circus*. This definitely qualifies her to write for children!

Published in Australia, UK, USA, & Europe, she has over 30 children's & education books with mainstream & digital publishers. Major awards include Children's Choice, NZ, Top Ten Children's & YA Books, NZ & Premier's Recommended Reading List, NSW.

J.R. loves teaching fun with words & doing dramatised book readings. She created a picture book in collaboration with Craig Smith, for a participatory audience at the Lockyer Festival.

Under J.R.McRae, she creates novels, award winning literary poetry, short stories & artworks. Her current adventures consist of global collaborations with other gifted creatives.

You can explore J.R's adventures here:

🌐 www.jenniferrpoulter.weebly.com/
www.jrmcrae_subversive.weebly.com

"Claudia Emanuela Coppola, born in Milan, Italy, is uniquely positioned as an artist, moving effortlessly across disciplines as a writer, painter, theatre director and illustrator.

Sinuous lines, vivid colors and sensational tones are characteristic of the faces she paints. The enchanting eyes of her young figures express an immense fragility, a sadness mixed with innocence. Trapped in their dreamy world, Coppola's figures have the power to open us to the soul with their glance.

Coppola has been widely recognized with awards and exhibitions in Madrid, Roma, Napoli, Milano, Torino, Taormina, Treviso, Budapest, Paris, London, Lisbon, Berlin, Barcelona and New Yourk." Christine Kennedy (New York)

Claudia can be contacted here:

 claudia.e.coppola@gmail.com

 /claudiaemanuelacoppola

 /wunderkammerbyme

Illustrator, Story Designer and Artist, Takara Beech illustrates and designs books from picture and middle grade books to Urban Aerial Yoga books. She is the co-creator of 13 books to be released in 2016 and 2017.

She has a Bachelor of Arts in Graphic Design and an illustration degree from the 'school of perseverance and forever learning.' Takara loves to inspire the imaginations of children and adults through her art and designs. She believes anyone can enjoy painting and the art of creation in a fun, holistic and healing way.

You can explore Takara's adventures here:

 www.takarabeech.com

 /takara.beech

 /takarabeech

www.ingramcontent.com/pod-product-compliance
Lightning Source LLC
Chambersburg PA
CBHW041539040426
42446CB00002B/153